ESG
Transforming Projects

Sustainable Practices for Impactful Results

Fabio Camatari

DEDICATION

To the sons and daughters of all readers of this book, may these
pages help to leave a legacy of hope and a better future.
To my son Benjamin and his future.

CONTENTS

ACKNOWLEDGMENTS

I am grateful to God for the opportunities He has presented to me throughout my life, which have paved the way for my professional and personal journey up to this point.

To my family, my wife Angelica, and my dear son Benjamin, for all the love and patience in sharing the space, routine, and challenges of working from home with me!

1 AUTHOR NOTES

ESG has arrived and is already knocking at our door!

This is my fourth editorial project and yet another project where I continue to assert that any project is indeed made by people. And I add: for people.

People have problems to be solved, not things. People have needs and expectations, not things. Focusing on people and solving their problems will make your project a true legacy.

And ESG has arrived, knocking at our door, at the project office. We started with the G for Governance (something always present in project management), then came the E for Environment, and finally, it's time for the S for Social and all its highly necessary load of Diversity, Equity, and Inclusion.

This book will guide you and bring together the content from various open documents, such as the P5 standard and the SDGs - Sustainable Development Goals, among other articles and guidelines that have been consulted over the past three years.

I hope you enjoy the reading and send me your comments!

2 PRESENTATION

This book aims to fill a gap in literature by addressing the intersection between ESG and Project Management. While awareness of the importance of sustainability is on the rise, there is still a shortage of comprehensive and practical resources that combine these two fields of knowledge. Our goal is to provide a solid and practical foundation for project management professionals who wish to drive sustainable transformation in their organizations.

By combining ESG principles with project management skills and knowledge, this book offers valuable insights on how to align business goals with sustainability objectives and effectively integrate responsible practices throughout the project lifecycle. Through case studies and best practices, we demonstrate that it is possible to achieve positive outcomes for both the project and society at large.

We hope this book serves as a source of inspiration and guidance for all those seeking to become agents of change, harnessing the power of project management to tackle the challenges of resource scarcity and promote a more sustainable future. I hope to contribute to a greater understanding and adoption of sustainable and responsible practices in project management, driving progress towards a more balanced and conscious world.

3 WHO IS THIS BOOK INTENDED FOR?

This book is intended for a wide range of professionals and individuals interested in ESG and project management. Among the potential readers are:

Project Management Professionals: Project managers, team leaders, and other professionals involved in the planning, execution, and monitoring of projects who wish to incorporate sustainable and responsible practices into their approaches.

Executives and Business Managers: CEOs, directors, and managers from organizations across sectors who seek to understand how to integrate ESG principles into their strategies and projects, driving sustainable growth and value creation for all stakeholders.

Sustainability Consultants: Consulting professionals and sustainability experts who wish to deepen their knowledge of how project management can be effectively applied to promote responsible practices within organizations.

Finance Professionals and Investors: Investors, financial analysts, and capital market professionals interested in understanding the relationship between ESG and project management to make more informed investment decisions and assess the sustainable performance of companies.

Students and Academics: University students and researchers seeking to explore the field of ESG and its relationship with project management, both as a field of study and as a practical application.

In summary, this book aims to cater to a diverse audience,

encompassing professionals from different sectors and hierarchical levels, as well as students and academics interested in the intersection between ESG and project management.

4 DEFINITIONS AND CONCEPTS ABOUT PROJECTS AND ESG

"A project is a temporary endeavor undertaken to create a unique product, service, or result."
"Project management is the application of knowledge, skills, tools, and techniques to project activities to meet the project requirements."

Both statements are the definitions of a project according to the PMBOK® Guide (Project Management Body of Knowledge).

Made by people: I often say that no matter how technological a project may be and how monolithic its deliverables are, a project is indeed made by people. And I add: for people. People have problems to be solved, not things. People have needs and expectations, not things. Focusing on people and solving their problems will make your project a true legacy.

Progressively elaborated: You don't sit down with a team in a meeting room and define the entire project plan in one morning, fueled by coffee and snacks. That can, at most, generate a high-level plan that needs to be detailed. A project is driven by iterations – a process of repeating one or more actions; it is the ability to do and redo, always seeking improvement.

Subject to constraints: Constraints are here to show us the limits, such as the available budget, expected time frame, quality standards, available resources, and others that each project or organization may present.

Has a start and end: Every project must have a beginning and an end. If you're involved in a project and the end date is not clear, "run,

Forest, run!" As the PMBOK itself describes, a project is a temporary endeavor.

Creates a unique outcome: The outcome can be a product, service, indicator, quality improvement, among other opportunities and objectives for a project. It is important to emphasize that it always delivers a unique outcome, something that didn't exist there before, for that group of people. No matter how repetitive the delivery of a technical solution, for example, the context will always be different.

Responsibilities of a project manager

An experienced project manager takes a systemic view of their project, considering all factors, internal and external, throughout the entire project lifecycle. Project managers are the ones who manage resource consumption in a project and can instill a lifecycle mindset into the project - from initiation to final disposal.

The PMI Code of Ethics and Professional Conduct states: "We make decisions and take actions based on the best interests of society, public safety, and the environment." This aspirational statement demonstrates the importance of balancing sustainability with other project management priorities.

Project management skills

The skills required to be a successful project manager are not mutually exclusive from other organizational skills. In other words, the competencies developed in other roles will be useful as a project manager. Similarly, the skills developed as a project manager can be transferred to other roles.

An effective comparison would be project management skills with those of a team manager. Although a project manager typically does not have direct subordinates, a team manager has a team of people reporting directly to them. The Venn diagram below provides a contrast between the roles and where they may intersect. While not intended as a standard comparison, it demonstrates that the skills of each role are different but complementary:

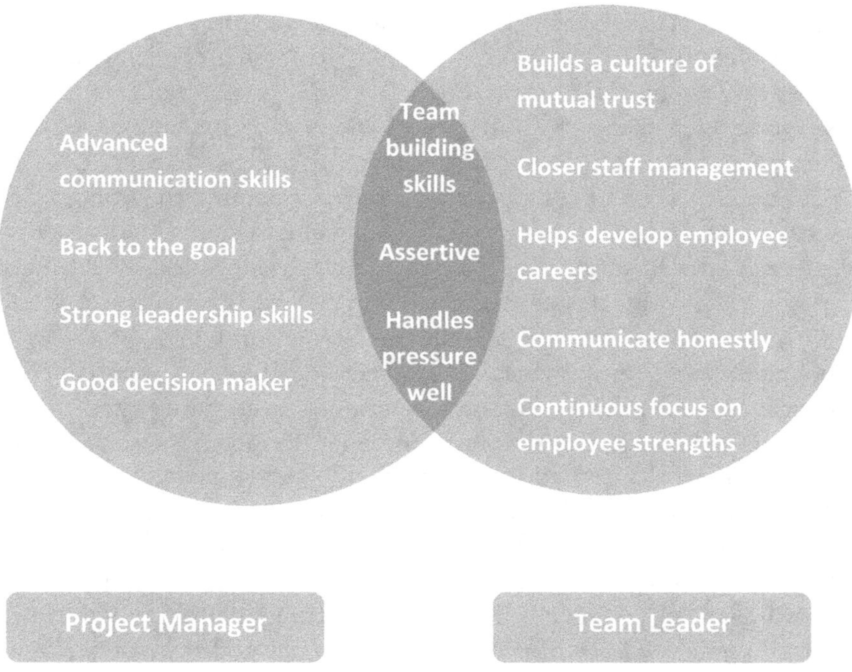

So, what does ESG have to do with project management?

Clearly, change is necessary, and projects are how we implement changes. Similarly, projects often impact sustainability both directly (by creating pollution or misusing resources) and indirectly (through the design of products and services they deliver).

A recent study by GPM, Insights on Sustainable Project Management, found that among the over one thousand executives surveyed, 96% believe that projects and project management are essential for sustainable development. 100% of these executives believe that project managers should understand the importance of sustainability for their projects.

Among project managers, 71% reported that the P5 Standard has improved sustainability in their projects. Among project managers actively using P5 in projects, 95% were able to realize greater sustainability benefits.

Definitions about ESG

ESG is an acronym for Environmental, Social, and Governance practices of an organization. The term was coined in 2004 in a publication by the Global Compact in partnership with the World Bank, called "Who Cares Wins." It emerged from a challenge by UN Secretary-General Kofi Annan to 50 CEOs of major financial institutions regarding the integration of social, environmental, and governance factors into the capital market. At the same time, UNEP-FI released the Freshfield report, which demonstrated the importance of integrating ESG factors for financial evaluation. In 2006, the PRI (Principles for Responsible Investment) was established, which now has over 3,000 signatories with assets under management exceeding USD 100 trillion – in 2019, the PRI grew by around 20%.

Understanding and applying ESG criteria by Brazilian companies is increasingly becoming a reality. Acting in accordance with ESG standards enhances the competitiveness of the business sector, both domestically and internationally. In today's world, where companies are closely monitored by their various stakeholders, ESG indicates solidity, lower costs, better reputation, and greater resilience amidst uncertainties and vulnerabilities.

According to the Climate Change and Sustainability Services from Ernest Young, ESG information is essential today for investors' decision-making. ESG criteria are fully related to the Sustainable Development Goals (SDGs), a reality in capital market discussions. The 17 Sustainable Development Goals encompass the major challenges and vulnerabilities of society as a whole. They indicate the key areas to be closely monitored and also signal significant opportunities when directly addressing those needs.

There are several widely recognized standards and guidelines that also address sustainability in projects, although they are not the focus of this book. However, we will provide the necessary references:

1. ISO 14001: This is an international standard for environmental management systems. Although applicable to any type of organization, it can be used to incorporate sustainability practices into projects.

2. LEED (Leadership in Energy and Environmental Design): It is a widely used certification system for sustainable buildings. While more focused on the construction and operation of buildings, many construction projects adopt its principles to promote sustainability.

3. GRI (Global Reporting Initiative): It is a reporting framework that assists organizations in measuring and

reporting their environmental, social, and governance performance. While not specifically focused on project management, it can be used to monitor and report the impact of projects on sustainability areas.

The UN's 2030 Agenda for Sustainable Development, while not a standard itself, establishes 17 Sustainable Development Goals (SDGs) and associated targets. Projects can align with these SDGs to contribute to broader sustainable development. This will be part of our scope as it aligns with the P5 Standard.

These are just some of the existing approaches and standards that aim to incorporate sustainability into projects. To better understand the mentioned P5 Standard, I suggest researching updated sources or contacting organizations and experts specific to the field of project management and sustainability.

What are the SDGs?

Designed for global action: Between 2000 and 2015, the Millennium Development Goals (MDGs) provided an important framework for development and achieved success in various areas, such as poverty reduction and improvements in health and education in developing countries.

The Sustainable Development Goals (SDGs) succeeded the MDGs, expanding the challenges to be addressed in eradicating poverty and incorporating a wide range of interrelated topics across the economic, social, and environmental dimensions of sustainable development.

The emergence of the SDGs is arguably the most inclusive process in the history of the United Nations, reflecting substantial input from all sectors of society and all parts of the world. Over 1,500 companies in the United Nations Global Compact alone have provided input and guidance.

The goals are universally applicable to both developing and developed nations. Governments are expected to translate them into national action plans, policies, and initiatives that reflect the different realities and capacities of their countries.

Although primarily targeted at governments, the SDGs are designed to bring together a wide range of organizations and shape priorities and aspirations for sustainable development efforts around a common framework. Most importantly, the SDGs recognize the leading role that businesses can and should play in achieving the goals. Below is a table with the 17 Sustainable Development Goals.

6
CLEAN WATER
AND SANITATION

12
RESPONSIBLE
CONSUMPTION
AND PRODUCTION

SUSTAINABLE
DEVELOPMENT
GOALS

5
GENDER
EQUALITY

11
SUSTAINABLE CITIES
AND COMMUNITIES

17
PARTNERSHIPS
FOR THE GOALS

4
QUALITY
EDUCATION

10
REDUCED
INEQUALITIES

16
PEACE, JUSTICE
AND STRONG
INSTITUTIONS

3
GOOD HEALTH
AND WELL-BEING

9
INDUSTRY, INNOVATION
AND INFRASTRUCTURE

15
LIFE
ON LAND

2
ZERO
HUNGER

8
DECENT WORK AND
ECONOMIC GROWTH

14
LIFE
BELOW WATER

1
NO
POVERTY

7
AFFORDABLE AND
CLEAN ENERGY

13
CLIMATE
ACTION

5 INCORPORATING ESG IN PROJECT MANAGEMENT PRACTICES

Human Resource Management
Proper Training and Supervision of Working Conditions

As project managers enhance skills, team interaction, and the overall team environment to improve project performance, they also need to look at the bigger picture - to look beyond the artificial barriers of the project itself and assess the implications of human resources on the broader community and throughout the product lifecycle that the project is creating.

Human resource elements often receive little attention from project managers, partly because most project teams operate in a matrix environment where team members do not report directly to the project manager. Therefore, the project manager primarily addresses human resource management through team formation, recognition and rewards, and occasionally the professional development of team members.

However, a long-term sustainable focus requires the project manager to address these elements for project team members:

- Work-life balance, training, personnel administration policies, meetings, and travel.
- Equity, quality, and appreciation of the work environment, education, ethics, skill development, and social inclusion.
- Adequate income for team members to economically support themselves and their families, family services, health and safety, labor rights, respect, transparency, and honesty.

This is a lot for a project manager, and much of it is beyond direct control but not outside their influence. By being aware of these issues, they can raise them directly with line management or address them as best they can within the project's boundaries.

However, their responsibility does not end there. There are also human resource management issues for the broader community of stakeholders. An organization cannot claim to have a sustainability focus if vendors and suppliers do not follow the same principles in developing raw materials that the purchasing organization adheres to.

Acquisition Management:

Sustainability Across the Value Chain Through Contract and Supplier Management

Project acquisition management includes the contract management and change control processes necessary to develop and administer contracts or purchase orders issued by authorized members of the project team.

Project managers are encouraged to consider the following when planning acquisition activities:

- Market conditions
- Products, services, and deliverables available in the market
- Suppliers, including past performance or reputation
- Typical terms and conditions for products, services, deliverables, or the specific industry
- Unique local requirements

However, the assessment doesn't stop there. In 2009, Walmart's private-label division tested seven existing products, asking suppliers to assess these products on four sustainability dimensions: resource usage, including non-renewable resources; impact on climate change; impact on ecosystems throughout the product's supply chain; and impact on human health. This pilot has since been extended to over 100,000 global suppliers as a crucial step in increasing supply chain transparency. The goal is to eventually provide this data to customers to aid in their purchasing decisions.

Project managers are advised that the complexity and level of detail in acquisition documents should be consistent with the value and risks associated with the planned acquisition. Project managers are accustomed to factoring risk into acquisition documents and using these documents to transfer risk to the supplier or otherwise manage it. However, these risks have traditionally been limited to the risks of the project itself and its schedule, cost, and scope constraints. If an organization is moving towards a sustainable and long-term vision of its business, it makes sense for these values to be reflected in procurement contracts as well, in areas such as bribery, child labor, and similar factors that may pose a risk to the company as a whole.

Operationally, organizations tend to view waste reduction as a solitary activity. However, it is only when integrated throughout the organization and project management that the organization begins to look at the entire supply chain and value chain - to reduce the quantity purchased to reduce the quantity wasted.

- Do supplier evaluations include sustainability criteria?
- Are sustainability obligations and commitments codified in contracts?
- How transparent is the entire supply chain in terms of sustainability priorities?

Risk Management: Incorporating Reputation and Social Risks into Risk Planning and Mitigation Strategies

As traditionally defined, risk is an uncertain event or condition that, if it occurs, will impact at least one project objective: scope, schedule, cost, or quality. However, if we look not only at the project implementation but also its effect throughout its entire lifecycle on the community and the organization as a whole, it becomes clear that we must examine risk more broadly.

Risks arising from environmental issues or social discontent around a project can be extremely costly in terms of delays and shutdowns, negative publicity, threats to operating licenses, and significant unforeseen expenses. At the same time, the damage to a company's reputation can far exceed the immediate cost impacts of a single project.

Just as other risk management categories cannot be prescriptive across all sectors, sustainability risks can vary significantly. Different core subjects and issues apply to different projects and industries. For example, extractive industries may have more environmental risks, while textile companies may have more risks in terms of social sustainability. To assess what is at stake, companies must examine the entire value chain, looking at how they source raw materials, manufacture and sell their products, for example.

In terms of sustainability risk approach, companies move from blind spots to awareness, compliance, and transparency. Many companies are satisfied with merely complying with laws or regulations, but enforcing compliance is the lowest level of engagement. Compliance implies that a company is meeting basic standards, not raising the bar for competitors and certainly not improving the lives of stakeholders. There is a huge difference between avoiding harm and actively pursuing good.

Increasingly, a company's long-term sources of value are affected by a growing wave of stakeholder expectations about the social role of businesses. The public understandably has the right to expect that companies fulfill their functions honorably within the social framework and play a conscientious role that earns public trust. Additionally, in an economy where 70% to 80% of market value comes from intangible assets that are difficult to assess, such as brand value, intellectual capital, and goodwill, organizations are particularly vulnerable to anything that damages their reputation. A company that has not invested in building a positive reputation through sustainability is susceptible to harm when negative stories arise, as there is no positive correlation in the consumer's mind to balance out the negative impacts of bad news.

The challenge is to find a way for companies to systematically incorporate awareness of sociopolitical issues into their key strategic decision-making processes. Companies must see social and political dimensions not only as risks—areas for damage limitation—but also as opportunities. They must scan the horizon for emerging trends and integrate their responses throughout the organization so that resulting initiatives are cohesive and not fragmented. In this way, the risk management process informs portfolio management and the overall strategic plan.

Communication Management: Sustainability Responsibilities

Project communication management includes the processes necessary to ensure the timely and appropriate generation, collection, distribution, storage, retrieval, and ultimate disposition of project information. Project managers spend most of their time communicating with team members and other project stakeholders. Effective communication creates a bridge among the diverse stakeholders involved in a project, connecting various cultural and organizational backgrounds, different levels of expertise, and multiple perspectives and interests in project execution or outcome.

Communications, encompassing project reports, presentations, records, and lessons learned, will ensure that project stakeholders are informed about the project's sustainability aspects.

Stakeholder management includes:

- Actively managing stakeholder expectations to increase the likelihood of project acceptance by negotiating and influencing their desires to achieve and maintain project goals.
- Addressing concerns that have not yet become issues, often related to anticipating future problems. These concerns need to be uncovered and discussed, and the risks need to be assessed.
- Clarifying and resolving identified issues. Resolution may result in a change request or may be dealt with outside the project, for example, deferred to another project or phase or deferred to another organizational entity.

Project managers should consider the following:

- How should the project communicate with stakeholders—activist groups, non-governmental organizations (NGOs), government agencies, or community members who want to know about the project and its impacts?
- How will information be received and processed from these stakeholders?
- How can we ensure engagement at the appropriate level?

Environment - Why Sustainability?

Humanity has been deceived by economic models that undervalue our natural resources. By economic models that jeopardize our ability to survive as a species. By economic models that consider profit as the sole indicator of business success.

Instead of these models, business leaders around the world are increasingly responding to the demands of investors, employees, and consumers to use models that reward low-carbon and environmentally sustainable products and services.

The driving force behind these demands is concern for the long-term viability of life as we know it in the face of human-induced climate change. Research has made it clear that the sixth mass extinction - the first since the Ordovician-Silurian Extinction approximately 439 million years ago, where 86% of life on Earth disappeared - is upon us. According to the proceedings of the United States National Academy of Sciences, nearly half of the 177 mammal species studied have lost more than 80% of their distribution between 1900 and 2015. The impacts, ecological factors, social, and economic factors associated with such a magnitude of biodiversity loss are unknown.

Sustainability is also necessary to address other global challenges, such as extreme poverty, inequality, and lack of access to quality education. Innovation and opportunity must be brought to the forefront to set the tone for an agile, progressive, and productive global economy.

By early August each year (soon to be late July), we humans will have consumed what the planet can regenerate. Between January and July, more carbon is emitted than forests and oceans can absorb throughout the year. We are overfishing, overextracting, and consuming freshwater excessively.

In total, we consume the natural resources of 1.7 Earths per year.

Earth Overshoot Day, the day we reach our consumption limit, is moving closer to January each year. It was first calculated in 1986 and fell in November. In 1993, it shifted to October, and in 2017, it was August 2nd. Some countries exceed their consumption limits much earlier. For example, the United Kingdom reaches its limit in early May. The only country that does not exceed its limits is Honduras.

One of the reasons for excessive consumption is the increasing world population. According to the United Nations Population Fund, there are over 7 billion people in the world, twice as many as in 1970 and four times as many as in 1910. In terms of net gain, we add 200,000 people to the planet every day, and according to projections, we are heading towards over 9 billion, which is unsustainable.

Excessive consumption has impacted our oceans by increasing acidification by over 30% since the beginning of the industrial revolution, according to the U.S. National Oceanic and Atmospheric

Administration. The increased levels of acidification caused the bleaching of the Great Barrier Reef in 2016 and 2017, the first time this happened in consecutive years. It takes ten years for the fastest-growing corals to recover, and the bleaching events...

Social

In a recent project, we spoke with 30 business leaders and identified that the main challenge for companies in the social aspect of ESG is precisely the relationship with the community surrounding the company, even before promoting diversity.

Social license to operate: Coined 25 years ago, the term "social license to operate" means the company has the approval of the community. Unlike an environmental permit, this social license is not formalized or calculated, but it is equally important.

The company must understand the demands, expectations, and needs of that community and plan its operation in a way that is advantageous to its surroundings, acting for the benefit of the population and local development.

First and foremost, it is necessary to understand that local actors and grassroots movements are already promoting social and economic development in their territories and understand better than anyone else the solutions that need to be implemented.

Therefore, companies must shed both a colonizing view that their actions in the territory will make all the difference and the belief that doing the bare minimum is enough to have a good relationship with the residents.

To promote the development of the territories in which they operate, it is important for companies to collaborate and coordinate with local organizations and leaders, as well as the government.

According to the Business Commitment Agenda for Sustainable Territorial Development by the Ethos Institute, both environmental actions such as the use of clean energy sources, emission and waste reduction, and management of water and land use and preservation, as well as social actions such as decent work generation, reducing inequalities, strengthening the local economy, improving quality of life, public health, and promoting educational opportunities, are necessary.

Governance

Governance is the establishment of rules and practices by which management ensures accountability, impartiality, agility, and transparency in the organization's relationships with its stakeholders. Governance can be subtle and may not be easily observable. Governance pertains to the culture and environment in which the organization and its stakeholders interact. Governance includes:

- Explicit agreements between the organization and its stakeholders for the distribution of responsibilities, rights, and rewards.
- Explicit agreements between the organization and its stakeholders regarding who is involved in activities and decisions and to what extent.
- Procedures to reconcile the sometimes conflicting interests of stakeholders in accordance with their duties, privileges, and functions.
- Supervision procedures, control, and adequate information flows that function as a system of checks and balances.

Good governance refers to the rules and practices for making and implementing decisions. It is not so much about making the right decisions but about defining and following the best possible process for making those decisions.

A good decision-making process and, therefore, good governance will have a positive effect on many aspects of the organization, including stakeholder engagement policies and practices, meeting procedures, service quality protocols, employee conduct, role definition, and good working relationships.

A good decision-making process will also help ensure that the organization acts prudently, lawfully, and ethically.

Effective governance encourages organizations to create value through innovation, development, and exploration, and provide accountability and control systems in line with the risks involved.

There are many effective approaches to good governance.

6 P5 APPROACH - PRODUCT, PROCESS, PEOPLE, PLANET, AND PROSPERITY

Product and Process Impacts

The main objective of P5 is to identify the potential sustainability impacts, both positive and negative, that can be analyzed and presented to management to support informed decisions and effective resource allocation.

The table below summarizes the P5 ontology. An ontology is a set of concepts and categories in a subject area that shows their properties and the relationships between them. An ontology helps manage complexity by organizing available information in a coherent manner. Sections 2 to 5 provide guidance on what the project team should do to support each element and what sustainable outcomes the team may be able to achieve.

The top level of the table represents the Triple Bottom Line of People, Planet, and Prosperity, including consideration of Product and Process impacts. Thus, P5 stands for Product, Process, People, Planet, and Prosperity.

Most people associate projects with the introduction stage, but in reality, most products will have support from multiple projects throughout their lifecycle. For example:

- A hotel may have many maintenance and upgrade projects during its lifespan.
- A passenger vehicle is usually updated annually with new features; each new version is created through one or more projects.
- Computer software is regularly updated with bug fixes and new features; each version is typically supported by one or more projects.

Ensuring sustainable production and consumption patterns. Enhanced sustainability throughout the product's lifecycle helps achieve the following sustainable project outcomes:
- Increased market differentiation and brand protection.
- Reduced environmental impact of the project.
- Reduced disposal costs.
- Lower risk and increased value and benefits over the product's lifespan.

Improved product maintenance helps achieve the following sustainable project outcomes:
- Increased market differentiation and brand protection.
- Reduced environmental impact of the project.

People (Social) Impacts

The People (Social) category of sustainability refers to the impacts that project activities and outcomes can have on individuals, society, and communities. The focus of the People category is to act ethically and maintain mutually beneficial relationships with employees, customers, suppliers, supply chains, and the community at large.
The People category contains the following subcategories:
- Labor practices and decent work
- Society and customers
- Human rights
- Ethical behavior

Ensuring healthy lives and promoting well-being for all ages. A safe and healthy workplace for the project team, which in turn results in a more engaged and committed team. Minimal time lost and minimal costs due to illnesses and workplace injuries.
Improved project health and safety help achieve the following sustainable project outcomes:
- A safe and healthy workplace for the project team, which in turn
- results in a more engaged and committed team.
- Minimal time lost and minimal costs due to illnesses and workplace injuries.
- Prevention of fines and penalties for health and safety law

violations.

Ensuring inclusive and equitable quality education and promoting lifelong learning opportunities for all. The project team should:
- Identify the necessary skills for the project.
- Identify skill gaps and development needs of project team members.
- Support and encourage project team members to pursue training and development.
- Train and mentor project team members to develop competence.

Improved local skills development helps achieve the following sustainable project outcomes:
- Local support for the project and product.
- Local support for future projects.
- Growth of the local economy.
- Achieving gender equality and empowering all women and girls.

Support for non-discrimination helps achieve the following sustainable project outcomes:
- Reduced costs through decreased absenteeism, increased productivity, and fostering a more motivated and committed team.
- Greater benefits from leveraging additional perspectives and insights.
- Improved reputation of the sponsoring organization.
- Promoting sustained, inclusive, and sustainable economic growth, full and productive employment, and decent work for all.

The project team should promote best labor and decent work practices, with actions focused on employment and recruitment, such as fair and equal wages, adequate employment conditions (healthcare, proper vacation, work-life balance, for example).
Reducing inequality within and among countries. Increased ability to attract highly qualified personnel. An engaged and motivated workforce that is committed to personal and organizational success.

This element encompasses the policies, procedures, and practices necessary to ensure that project personnel do not experience discrimination for any reason.

The project team should:

- Provide equal opportunities for all based on ability.
- Show zero tolerance for biases based on age, gender, ethnicity, and other aspects of diversity.
- Maximize the skills and experience of project team members in problem-solving.

Support for diversity and equal opportunities helps achieve the following sustainable project outcomes:

- Reduced recruitment costs by being known as a preferred employer.
- Creation of innovative solutions to problems due to the diverse background of project team members.

Compliance with public policies helps achieve the following sustainable project outcomes:

- Increased transparency and accountability.
- Protection of the sponsoring organization's reputation and brand.
- Increased community support.
- Reduced risk.

Making cities and human settlements inclusive, safe, resilient, and sustainable. Community support helps achieve the following sustainable project outcomes:

- Acceptance of the project outcome and improved realization of benefits.
- Improved relationship between the sponsoring organization and the community.

Protection of indigenous peoples helps achieve the following sustainable project outcomes:

- Ensuring the long-term existence of indigenous and tribal lands, cultures, religions, and ways of life.
- Increased trust from potential employees.
- Improved reputation of the sponsoring organization.

Promoting peaceful and inclusive societies for sustainable development, providing access to justice for all, and building effective, accountable, and inclusive institutions at all levels.
The project team should:

- Support the ILO Minimum Age Convention.
- Ensure that all workers meet or exceed the minimum age required by law.
- Avoid placing children in situations that may harm their health or general well-being.
- Protect the human rights, including the right to education, of all child workers.
- Demand the same from suppliers and their supply chains.

Elimination of bribery and corruption helps achieve the following sustainable project outcomes:

- Strengthened market presence and brand reputation.
- Reduced risk of legal proceedings.
- Reduced recruitment costs and higher employee retention rates.

Strengthening the means of implementation and revitalizing the global partnership for sustainable development. This element encompasses the policies, procedures, and practices necessary to ensure that true and accurate information about project activities and outcomes is shared with affected individuals and organizations.
The project team should:

- Disclose the project's support for sustainability.
- Avoid making irrational, misleading, or false claims about project activities or outcomes.
- Correct any misinformation as quickly as possible.

Improved market communications and advertising help achieve the following sustainable project outcomes:

- Increased customer loyalty.
- Greater community support.
- Increased market value and shareholder value.
- Improved reputation of the sponsoring organization.

Product and Process Impacts

The main goal of P5 is to identify the possible sustainability impacts, both positive and negative, that can be analyzed and presented to management to support informed decisions and effective resource allocation.

The table below summarizes the P5 ontology. An ontology is a set of concepts and categories in a subject area that shows their properties and relationships. An ontology helps manage complexity by organizing available information coherently. Sections 2 to 5 provide guidance on what the project team should do to support each element and the sustainable outcomes the team may achieve.

The top level of the table represents the Triple Bottom Line of People, Planet, and Prosperity, including consideration of Product and Process impacts. Thus, P5 stands for Product, Process, People, Planet, and Prosperity.

PROJECT										
Product Impacts				**Process (Project Management) Impacts**						
Lifespan of Product		Servicing of Product		Effectiveness of Project Processes		Efficiency of Project Processes		Fairness of Project Processes		
People (Social) Impacts				**Planet (Environmental) Impacts**				**Prosperity (Economic) Impacts**		
Labor Practices and Decent Work	Society and Customers	Human Rights	Ethical Behavior	Transport	Energy	Land, Air, and Water	Consumption	Business Case Analysis	Business Agility	Economic Stimulation
Employment and Staffing	Community Support	Non-discrimination	Procurement Practices	Local Procurement	Energy Consumption	Biological Diversity	Recycling and Reuse	Modeling and Simulation	Flexibility/ Optionality	Local Economic Impact
Labor/Management Relations	Public Policy/ Compliance	Age-Appropriate Labor	Anti-Corruption	Digital Communication	CO2 Emissions	Water and Air Quality	Disposal	Present Value	Business Flexibility	Indirect Benefits
Project Health and Safety	Protection for Indigenous & Tribal Peoples	Voluntary Labor	Fair Competition	Traveling and Commuting	Clean Energy Return	Water Consumption	Contamination and Pollution	Direct Financial Benefits		
Training and Education	Customer Health and Safety			Logistics	Renewable Energy	Sanitary Water Displacement	Waste Generation	Return on Investment		
Organizational Learning	Product and Service Labeling							Benefit-Cost Ratio		
Diversity and Equal Opportunity	Mkt. Comm. and Advertising							Internal Rate of Return		
Local Competence Development	Customer Privacy									

Most people associate projects with the introduction stage, but in reality, most products will be supported by multiple projects throughout their lifecycle.

For example:

- A hotel can have many maintenance and upgrade projects during its lifespan.
- A passenger vehicle is usually updated annually with new features; each new version is created through one or more projects.
- Computer software is regularly updated with bug fixes and new features; each version usually relies on the support of one or more projects.

Ensuring sustainable production and consumption standards. Enhanced sustainability throughout the product's lifespan helps achieve the following sustainable project outcomes:

- Increased market differentiation and brand protection.
- Decreased environmental impact of the project.
- Reduction in disposal costs.
- Reduced risk and increased value and benefits throughout the product's lifespan.

Improved product maintenance helps achieve the following sustainable project outcomes:

- Increased market differentiation and brand protection.
- Decreased environmental impact of the project.

Social Impacts on People

The people (social) category of sustainability concerns the impacts that a project's activities and outcomes can have on individuals, society, and communities. The focus of the people category is to act ethically and maintain mutually beneficial relationships with employees, customers, suppliers, supply chains, and the community at large.

The people category includes the following subcategories:

- Labor practices and decent work
- Society and customers
- Human rights
- Ethical behavior

Ensuring a healthy life and promoting well-being for all, at all ages. A safe and healthy workplace for the project team, which in turn results in a more engaged and committed team. Minimum time lost and minimal costs associated with workplace illnesses and injuries.

Improved project health and safety contribute to the following sustainable project outcomes:

- A safe and healthy workplace for the project team, which in turn results in a more engaged and committed team.
- Minimum time lost and minimal costs associated with workplace illnesses and injuries.
- Prevention of fines and penalties for violations of health and safety laws and regulations.

Ensuring inclusive and equitable quality education and promoting lifelong learning opportunities for all. The project team should:

- Identify the skills needed for the project.
- Identify skill gaps and development needs of project team members.
- Support and encourage project team members to pursue training and development.
- Train and guide project team members to develop competence.

The development of local skills contributes to the following sustainable project outcomes:

- Local support for the project and the product.
- Local support for future projects.
- Growth of the local economy.
- Achieving gender equality and empowering all women and girls.

Supporting non-discrimination contributes to the following sustainable project outcomes:

- Reduced costs through reduced absenteeism, increased productivity, and fostering a more motivated and committed team.
- Greater benefits from leveraging additional perspectives and insights.

- Improved reputation of the sponsoring organization.
- Promoting sustained, inclusive, and sustainable economic growth, full and productive employment, and decent work for all.

The project team should promote best labor and decent work practices, with actions focused on employment and recruitment, such as fair and equal wages, appropriate employment conditions (healthcare, adequate vacation, work-life balance, etc.).

Reducing inequality within and among countries. Increased ability to attract highly qualified personnel. An engaged and motivated workforce committed to personal and organizational success. This element encompasses the policies, procedures, and practices necessary to ensure that project personnel do not experience discrimination for any reason.

The project team should:

- Offer equal opportunities for all based on ability.
- Show zero tolerance for biases based on age, gender, ethnicity, and other aspects of diversity.
- Maximize the skills and experience of project team members in problem-solving.

Supporting diversity and equal opportunity contributes to the following sustainable project outcomes:
- Reduced recruitment costs by being known as a preferred employer.
- Creation of innovative solutions to problems due to the diverse backgrounds of project team members.

Compliance with public policies contributes to the following sustainable project outcomes:
- Increased transparency and accountability.
- Protection of the sponsoring organization's reputation and brand.
- Greater community support.
- Reduced risk.

Making cities and human settlements inclusive, safe, resilient, and sustainable. Community support contributes to the following sustainable project outcomes:

- Acceptance of the project outcome and improved realization of benefits.
- Improved relationship between the sponsoring organization and the community.

Protecting indigenous and tribal peoples contributes to the following sustainable project outcomes:

- Ensuring the long-term existence of indigenous and tribal lands, cultures, religions, and ways of life.
- Increased trust from potential employees.
- Improved reputation of the sponsoring organization.

Promoting peaceful and inclusive societies for sustainable development, providing access to justice for all, and building effective, accountable, and inclusive institutions at all levels.
The project team should:

- Support the International Labour Organization's Convention on Minimum Age.
- Ensure that all workers meet or exceed the minimum age required by law.
- Prevent children from being placed in situations that could harm their health or general well-being.
- Protect the human rights, including the right to education, of all child workers.
- Demand the same from suppliers and their supply chains.

The elimination of bribery and corruption contributes to the following sustainable project outcomes:

- Reinforcement of market presence and brand reputation.
- Reduced risks of legal proceedings.
- Reduced recruitment costs and higher employee retention rates.

Strengthening the means of implementation and revitalizing the global partnership for sustainable development. This element encompasses the policies, procedures, and practices necessary to ensure that true and accurate information about project activities and outcomes is shared with affected individuals and organizations.

The project team should:

- Communicate the project's support for sustainability.
- Avoid making irrational, misleading, or false claims about project activities or outcomes.
- Correct any incorrect information as quickly as possible.

Improved market communications and advertising contribute to the following sustainable project outcomes:

- Increased customer loyalty.
- Greater community support.
- Increased market value and shareholder value.
- Improved reputation of the sponsoring organization.

Environmental Impacts on the Planet

The planet (environmental) category of sustainability concerns the impacts that a project's activities and outcomes can have on living and non-living natural systems.

These systems include land, air, and water, as well as the flora, fauna, and people who depend on them. The focus of the planet category is on preserving, restoring, and enhancing these natural systems.

The planet (environmental) category includes the following subcategories:

- Transportation
- Energy
- Land, Air, and Water
- Consumption

Ensuring the availability and sustainable management of water and sanitation for all. Increased awareness of water and air quality contributes to the following sustainable project outcomes:

- Preservation of local water bodies, such as lakes, ponds, rivers, and streams.
- Preservation of local ecosystems and the groundwater systems that sustain them.
- Prevention of water-related diseases.
- Improved air quality.

Reducing water consumption contributes to the following sustainable project outcomes:
- Reduced project costs for water use and treatment.
- Decreased environmental damage from the project.

Improved management of sanitary water displacement contributes to the following sustainable project outcomes:
- Prevention of water-related diseases and insect infestations.

Ensuring access to reliable, sustainable, modern, and affordable energy for all. Reducing CO_2 emissions contributes to the following sustainable project outcomes:
- Improved air quality.
- Improved health and well-being of project team members, the local community, and other stakeholders.
- Reduced emissions both during the project and throughout the product's lifecycle.

Clean energy return contributes to the following sustainable project outcomes:
- Energy returned to the power grid.
- Secondary energy sources provided to the local community.
- Reduced stress on the power grid.
- The use of renewable energy contributes to the following sustainable project outcomes:
- Improved brand reputation.
- Reduced risk of energy price fluctuations and supply shortages.
- Reduced impact on the causes of climate change.

Building resilient infrastructure, promoting inclusive and sustainable industrialization, and fostering innovation. Digital communication contributes to the following sustainable project outcomes:
- Time and cost savings through reduced travel.
- Ability to hire the best people for the job regardless of location.
- Reduced stress from long-distance travel and extended

periods away from home.
- Reduced CO2 emissions from transportation.

Ensuring sustainable production and consumption standards. The project team should:
- Actively seek local suppliers.
- Give preference to local suppliers whenever possible.

Local sourcing contributes to the following sustainable project outcomes:
- Support for the growth of the local economy.
- Reduced CO2 emissions from transportation.

Responsible recycling and reuse contribute to the following sustainable project outcomes:
- Reduced impact on natural resources by decreasing the need for raw materials.
- Reinforcement of brand reputation by promoting the use of responsibly sourced supplies and materials.
- Reduced disposal costs by minimizing waste.

Responsible disposal contributes to the following sustainable project outcomes:
- New or additional revenue streams through the use of unnecessary resources by third parties in support of a circular economy.
- Prevention of diseases from contamination.
- Minimal contamination of ecosystems.

Limiting waste generation contributes to the following sustainable project outcomes:
- Reduced project costs.
- Reduced environmental impact.
- Reduced disposal costs for undesirable, toxic, or hazardous substances.

Taking urgent action to combat climate change and its impacts. Improved logistics contribute to the following sustainable project outcomes:

- Reduced transportation costs.
- Waste reduction.
- Shorter lead times for essential components and products.
- Reduction or elimination of non-recyclable packaging.

Conservation and sustainable use of oceans, seas, and marine resources for sustainable development. Protection of biodiversity contributes to the following sustainable project outcomes:

- Healthy ecosystems that protect potential food, fiber, medicine, and other resources.
- Future access to land and other natural resources.
- Improved reputation among regulators and in local communities that rely on biodiversity in areas affected by the project.
- Continuous availability of ecosystem services such as air regulation, nutrient cycling, and pollination.

Protecting, restoring, and promoting sustainable use of terrestrial ecosystems, sustainably managing forests, combating desertification, halting and reversing land degradation, and halting biodiversity loss.

(Economic) Impacts on Prosperity

Projects have the power to make the world better, but strategic planning is needed to truly make a difference. Companies can't just say they are doing well. They need proof to support it. And it's not something nice to have. It's a matter of business survival. A simple project can have several "secondary" impacts upon its implementation:

- Creating new jobs.
- Improving internet access.
- Advancing inclusion.
- Building essential infrastructure.
- Boosting public health.

Young people, in particular, have embraced the cause, with about 3 in 4 millennials and Gen Z saying they plan to take action to positively impact their communities, according to a 2020 Deloitte survey. And that is leading to their work.
Positive action requires strong collaboration. And it starts with

listening. According to Pulse data, 69% of organizations that measure social impact do so in part through meetings with stakeholders.

This type of engagement with people can reveal opportunities to offer broader benefits on many fronts – sometimes with just one project. A company launching a large infrastructure project, for example, may choose to invest in a training program as a way to add value to local stakeholders and gain their support. But project leaders and their teams should not make assumptions.

The (economic) category of prosperity sustainability concerns the impacts that a project's activities and outcomes can have on the finances of project stakeholders. The focus of the prosperity category is to maximize positive returns for as many stakeholders as possible.

The prosperity category contains the following subcategories:

- Business plan analysis
- Business agility
- Economic stimulation

Return on Investment (ROI) is used to evaluate the expected financial return on money spent on a project. ROI is calculated using the following formula:

$$ROI = (Direct\ Financial\ Benefits - Project\ Costs)\ /\ Project\ Costs.$$

ROI is typically expressed as a percentage (i.e., if the gross calculation results in a value of 0.32, the ROI is expressed as 32%). Both numbers should reflect the present value as described above.

Ending poverty in all its forms, everywhere. Greater flexibility/optionality helps achieve the following sustainable project outcomes:

- Higher degree of success.
- Identification of opportunities to improve social and environmental impacts.
- Realization of superior benefits.

Increased business flexibility helps achieve the following sustainable project outcomes:

- Higher chance of project success.
- Enhanced ability to implement improvements.

- Competitive advantages for the organization.
- Greater potential to effectively respond to changes.

Awareness of local economic impact helps achieve the following sustainable project outcomes:
- Creation of local employment opportunities.
- Provision of additional economic benefit from money spent in the local economy.
- Potential for a better standard of living for people residing in the local community.
- Tax revenue for the community in support of services and infrastructure.
- Support for a cycle of prosperity.

Recognition of the importance of indirect benefits helps achieve the following sustainable project outcomes:
- Ownership and focus on achieving benefits.
- Added justification for the value and benefits of the project.
- Support for similar projects in the future.

Most common applications of the P5 Standard for Sustainability in Project Management

It is important to note that project leaders and their teams need to understand the Business Case well to apply this process. Additionally, it is essential to have a good understanding of project details, such as its objective, relevant requirements, and, most importantly, the organization's goals and strategies. The documentation of the P5 standard highlights that while the business case and project objective are the responsibility of the project owner, it is the project manager's role to collect, document, and reach an agreement on the requirements based on the understanding of the organizational strategy.

An important activity when conducting P5 impact analysis is to create a risk register. Depending on the project management methodology used, the format of this register may vary, but it should essentially contain essential information about the different types of risks associated with the project. As an example, we can mention the PMBOK, which is perhaps the most well-known guide to good practices in project management. It suggests the development of a Risk Management Plan, which identifies, analyzes, and proposes solutions or measures to minimize perceived and potential project risks. A risk management plan is a document that shows how to complete the project within an acceptable risk level, as established by the organization's values. Therefore, if sustainability is an important value for the organization, it is essential that the risk management plan aligns with that goal.

By applying the P5 standard, project managers can ensure that sustainability considerations are integrated into all phases of a project's lifecycle, from initiation to completion. This approach helps create projects that are more environmentally and socially responsible, taking into account the triple bottom line - people, planet, and profit. To apply the P5 standard - Green Project Management to traditional project management, you can follow the following steps:

Awareness: Start by creating awareness about the importance of sustainability in project management. Educate the project team and stakeholders about the principles and benefits of the P5 standard.

Initial assessment: Conduct an initial assessment to identify aspects of the project that can be improved in terms of sustainability. This may involve analyzing environmental, social, and economic factors related to the project.

Definition of sustainable goals: Based on the initial assessment, set clear and measurable sustainable goals that align with the principles of the P5 standard. For example, establish goals to reduce carbon emissions, minimize waste, or increase inclusion and diversity in the project.

Integration of sustainable practices: Identify relevant sustainable practices that can be integrated into the project. This may include the use of eco-friendly materials, implementation of energy-saving practices, proper waste management, promotion of gender equality, and more.

Stakeholder involvement: Involve relevant stakeholders throughout the process. Promote open communication and collaboration, encouraging the sharing of ideas and perspectives related to the project's sustainability.

Continuous monitoring and evaluation: Establish mechanisms to regularly monitor and evaluate progress towards the established sustainable goals. This will help identify areas that need adjustments or improvements and allow for course correction, if needed.

Communication and dissemination: Share the results and achievements related to the project's sustainability with internal and external stakeholders. This may include sustainability reports, relevant certifications, and transparent communication about implemented sustainable practices.

Remember that the application of the P5 standard - Green Project Management may vary depending on the nature and scope of each project. It is important to adapt practices and approaches according to specific needs, while always focusing on integrating sustainability principles throughout the project's lifecycle.

Incorporating sustainability into all functions

Factors by which good environmental, social, and governance management can contribute to value creation for shareholders, yes, those who will one day finance our projects:
- Early identification of emerging risks, threats, and management failures.
- New business opportunities.
- Customer satisfaction and loyalty, both internal and external.
- Reputation as an attractive employer.
- Alliances and partnerships with business partners and stakeholders.
- Improved reputation and brands.
- Reduction of regulatory intervention.
- Cost savings.
- Access to capital, lower cost of capital.
- Better risk management, lower risk levels.

Based on interviews conducted by GPM Global, these six trends are likely to continue, if not accelerate, after the pandemic:

Enhanced health and well-being initiatives: With a focus on mental health and stress reduction. McKinsey's report on the Future of Work found that at least 49% of remote workers are experiencing symptoms of burnout. This is an alarming proportion, signaling that productivity gains may not be lasting unless project managers take steps to support the psychological well-being of their teams.

Remote teams and hybrid meetings: A recent Gartner survey showed that 48% of employees are likely to work remotely at least part of the time after COVID-19, compared to 30% before the pandemic. Even with people returning to the office, project team meetings are likely to maintain a hybrid element that allows for full remote participation.

Personal growth and development: Maintaining work-life balance during quarantine has proven challenging for many, as the boundaries between personal and professional life have become even more blurred. Using free time to work on personal development, as well as practicing mindfulness, improves quality of life.

Emphasis on impact: The command and conquer approach to project delivery is giving way to a values and benefits-focused approach, and this will continue until impact is given equal importance to profitability.

Purpose over profit: While no one questions the need for profitability, organizations must put principles, values, and ethics at the center of the decision-making process to contribute to regenerative development.

Resilience: Organizations must develop resilience by establishing resilient governance, reviewing and rethinking crisis management structures and response strategies, while promoting a culture of resilience. This begins with breaking down silos between teams and integrating them to coordinate the tactics, tools, and technologies needed for effective crisis response.

7 PROJECT MANAGEMENT AND THE ENVIRONMENT

Project management must take action on the climate crisis.

Climate change is the defining crisis of our time, and its impacts are being recognized and felt in numerous ways all over the world. Rising temperatures are fueling environmental degradation, natural disasters, extreme weather events, food and water insecurity, economic disruptions, conflicts, and environmental refugees. Sea levels are rising, Arctic and Antarctic ice sheets are melting, coral reefs are dying, oceans are acidifying, forests are burning, and businesses and projects are being affected. Extreme and more frequent climate events are the most direct way to experience climate change in our daily lives.

In 2021 alone, the effects of just 10 climate events, including Hurricane Ida, floods in Europe, the winter storm in Texas, floods in Henan, China, floods in British Columbia, and a once-in-a-millennium heat dome, resulted in $170 billion in direct destruction. This doesn't even account for the disruption they and other extreme weather events had on business operations and projects due to capacity loss, increased costs, and reconstruction.

When asked, "Have extreme weather events such as flash floods, wildfires, sea-level rise affected your project work?" 38% of Project Managers said yes, compared to only 4% in 2019. The response was even higher among Program and Portfolio Managers, with 42% reporting impacts. Among executives, 28% said yes, while 72% were unsure or said no. When asked if the project profession is doing enough to address climate change, 100% said no.

There is no doubt that every profession must invest in and work to understand its impact on climate change and take immediate action to eliminate harmful practices. Business as usual is not good enough, and as the infinite cost of climate change reaches irreversible levels, now is the time for bold collective action in assessing the impact of projects and project work.

In addition to using our P5 Standard for Sustainability in Project Management, conducting a P5 Impact Analysis, and incorporating a Sustainability Management Plan into the project, answering a few simple questions can ensure balance:

1. Does my action heal the future or steal from it?
2. Does it increase or decrease human well-being?
3. Does it restore or deplete biodiversity?
4. Does it increase or decrease global warming?
5. Does it meet human needs or manufacture human wants?

Sustainability is the minimum, and that is not enough. Since 2009, GPM has been working to promote sustainable practices in project management. Our approach has always been to go beyond the common understanding of sustainability and focus on value creation, the central focus of regeneration.

According to Merriam Webster, sustainable is defined as "capable of being sustained" and "of, relating to, or being a method of harvesting or using a resource so that the resource is not depleted or permanently damaged." This simply isn't good enough. Our methods and tools advocate for addressing the root causes of sustainability-related problems and focusing on value creation, while the common understanding is merely "do no harm" but not necessarily "do good."

In practice, we have advocated for regeneration since our inception, which Paul Hawken eloquently describes in his new book, "Regeneration: Ending the Climate Crisis in One Generation," by putting life at the center of every action and decision.

The challenge of introducing new or different terminology (Regeneration vs. Sustainability) is that it took 30 years for sustainability to become a familiar term. Detractors might see it as just a repackaging of the old. In reality, regeneration goes beyond sustainability in decision-making that puts life first. Ultimately, we must ask ourselves, "What are we sustaining?" We must regenerate what has been lost and sustain that regenerated future state. To put it mildly, sustainability is the lowest rung on the ladder; we must aim higher.

Whether you choose to use Green, Sustainable, or Regenerative, your action is what matters.

Greenwashing

Consumer concern about environmental issues has grown significantly in recent years, and as a result, companies are also paying more attention to marketing their image as "environmentally friendly." However, it's important to note that in certain cases, this new "green" discourse from companies is not accompanied by real changes in internal practices and processes.

The market has good reasons to closely monitor changes in consumer profiles and adapt to them. The problem arises when a company manipulates information to present an environmentally responsible image to the public but is merely greenwashing or, to use the correct term, greenwashing.

Seven sins of greenwashing defined by the Canadian agency TerraChoice:

1. No Proof: Environmental claims that cannot be substantiated by readily accessible information or by a reliable third-party certification. Common examples include facial tissues or toilet paper claiming various percentages of post-consumer recycled content without providing evidence.
2. Hidden Trade-off: An environmental claim that is based on a narrow set of attributes, without attention to other important environmental issues. For example, paper is not necessarily environmentally preferable just because it comes from sustainably harvested forests. Other important environmental issues in the paper manufacturing process, such as greenhouse gas emissions or chlorine use in bleaching, may be equally important.

3. Vagueness and Imprecision: An environmental claim that is so poorly defined or broad that its real meaning is likely to be misunderstood by the consumer. "All-natural" is one example. Arsenic, uranium, mercury, and formaldehyde are natural. "All-natural" is not necessarily "green."

4.   Irrelevance: An environmental claim that may be true but is unimportant or does not help consumers seeking environmentally preferable products. "CFC-free" is a common example, as it is a frequent claim despite CFCs being banned by law.

5.   Lesser of Two Evils: An environmental claim that may be true within the product category but that distracts the consumer from the larger environmental impacts of the category as a whole. Organic cigarettes could be an example of this sin, as well as low fuel-consumption SUVs.

6.   Fibbing: Environmental claims that are simply false.

7.   Worshiping False Labels: A product that, through words or images, gives the impression of third-party endorsement that does not exist. In other words, fake labels.

How to avoid greenwashing practices

Given the common greenwashing practices mentioned earlier, it's possible to be alert to certain terms. However, there are some recommended behaviors for consumers interested in avoiding greenwashing:

Stay away from vague claims: Don't trust products with vague environmental claims such as "eco-friendly," "sustainable," or "environmentally friendly." Broad and vague terms like these are not allowed on product packaging according to the ABNT ISO 14021 standard. If you encounter them, it's greenwashing.

It looks like a seal, but it's not: It's common to come across images and designs that resemble seals but are actually a marketing ploy by the company. If you've never seen that symbol before, be suspicious and do some research! Many companies use symbols that resemble seals but are created by the company itself, giving a misleading impression of independent third-party certification.

Actions speak louder than words: Many companies put

recommendations and suggestions on their packaging, such as "Preserve the Environment, it thanks you," "Save water," or "Please recycle this packaging." However, the company lacks a socio-environmental policy and actions focused on the sustainability of their products. Responsibility for the environment lies with both the consumer and the company. It's common to find cases where consumers want to recycle the product's packaging, but the manufacturer hasn't invested in 100% recyclable or biodegradable packaging, making it difficult to do so. There are also cases where the company asks consumers to save water, but the company itself doesn't practice water reuse, resource optimization, or even rationing. When you encounter these messages on packaging, research the company's practices and socio-environmental policy, and if there is a lack of evidence, demand changes!

Don't rely solely on the company's word: It's not enough for a manufacturer to declare that their product is vegan, not tested on animals, saves 70% water, and is 100% biodegradable—they need to provide concrete evidence to support these claims. The ABNT NBR ISO 14021 standard, which deals with environmental labels and self-declarations, establishes that environmental declarations must ensure the reliability/validity of information and have a clear, transparent, scientifically sound, and documented methodology. If you come across an environmental self-declaration and want to confirm its veracity, contact the company's Customer Service (the email or phone number should be provided on the label) and request concrete evidence for such claims!

Follow organizations concerned with the cause: There are many civil society organizations, like Idec, that work on the issue of greenwashing and the socio-environmental responsibility of companies and are a reliable source for your research. Additionally, various independent international certifying bodies' websites provide content verifying such claims.

Six ways to incorporate sustainability into projects

Dealing with climate change is everyone's responsibility, from the cafeteria to the C-suite. However, making sustainability initiatives part of "business as usual" has proven challenging for many companies. The PMI's Global Megatrends 2022 report provides a detailed view of how the Climate Crisis is causing organizations to rethink and reequip their business models to adopt sustainable practices.

According to the PMI's Pulse of the Profession®: Why Social Impact Matters, to make sustainability a strategic priority, teams need an action plan and must measure their efforts with concrete data.

Six success factors emerged from this research as critical to sustainability projects:

1. Engage local stakeholders: This often requires a cultural shift and the ability to facilitate change and create economic incentives and value for the community or region that a project will impact.

2. Adopt a zero-waste approach: Nishita Baliarsingh, co-founder and CEO of Nexus Power in India, says that if you look at natural processes, there is nothing wasted. It comes from the land, goes back to the land—everything is circular. It's completely closed.

3. Examine every component of the value chain: Baliarsingh points out that looking at the complete life cycle of a sustainable product—from sourcing to production, distribution, and disposal—will likely reveal that it is not as sustainable as expected or doesn't have much impact.

4. Understand that trade-offs between people, the planet, and profit are not necessary: also according to Nishita Baliarsingh, sustainability is typically the optimized use of resources, and it's not like you're doing that for the planet and forgetting everything else. In terms of sustainable business, you go from raw material to consumer to disposal. Once you have a complete channel, the economy will improve.

5. Conduct a comprehensive risk assessment to ensure desired outcomes are achieved: Even a seemingly simple project like planting trees has many facets to consider, including safety, government regulations, stakeholder and community management, water supply, and biodiversity impact.

6. Invest in technology: This may be the only way to turn the

tide on climate change. New technologies, such as direct air capture and carbon mineralization, may one day remove carbon on the necessary scale.

By incorporating these practices, project professionals and teams have the ability to make a more sustainable and green world a reality.

Common Sustainability and Project Management Goals

Companies compete by constantly changing to meet market forces. These changes are primarily implemented through projects adopted by the organization.

So far, project management has been treated as an isolated island within the organization. Just as a project has discrete start and end points, it's as if a fortress has been built around it in terms of long-term impacts. Project managers only assess the risks that affect the project implementation itself, not the larger community or the company's reputation.

Companies have never been isolated from social or political expectations. The difference now is the intensification of pressure and the increasing complexity of these forces, the speed at which they change, and the activists' ability to mobilize public opinion. The business world is not only global but also swirling in a dynamic and turbulent environment. These seismic shifts in organizational thinking require project management to be more business-context-oriented, not just myopic about the project itself.

Incorporating sustainability into project management helps us deal with project complexity, reduces crisis situations, project cancellations and interruptions, and project personnel fluctuations. It creates a competitive advantage, economic benefits, and promotes sustainable project outcomes.

Gregory Balestrero, the former president of PMI, emphasized the significance of social responsibility, stating that it is no longer a choice driven by environmentally conscious CEOs. It has evolved into a mandatory commitment for all organizations across their operations. Project managers must acknowledge and fulfill this mandate both now and in the future.

8 PROJECT MANAGEMENT AND SOCIETY

Diversity, Equity, and Inclusion

Diversity: It refers to the plurality of individuals in terms of cultural differences, identity, experiences, and values that are shared throughout social and professional life. In other words, it encompasses the coexistence of people who are different in terms of ethnicity, sexual orientation, culture, gender, etc., in all areas and hierarchical levels of the company.

Equity: It is social justice, which means providing the necessary resources so that all individuals can start from the same starting point. If we intend to unite diverse life stories and contexts, with different perceptions, backgrounds, and needs, we cannot assume that everyone should receive equal treatment, but rather equitable treatment! That is, according to their specific needs.

Inclusion: It is the sense of belonging. Creating an environment in which all individuals can feel included and thrive. An inclusive company is one that develops strategies to embrace diversity and ensure that these individuals have equitable opportunities for growth in a safe environment within the company. And how do we achieve that? By preparing the environment to make people feel welcome. To make them perceive that the company and the team have made an effort to receive them and, most importantly, that they are respected and know how to engage with them.

Take advantage of diversity as you courageously venture into uncharted territory!

When Gene Roddenberry assembled the USS Enterprise with a highly diverse array of races, species, and genders, he used Star Trek as a platform to challenge the prevalent social injustices of the late 1960s. However, in doing so, he also unlocked another benefit of diversity: enhanced risk management.

The original mission of the Enterprise embodies many characteristics of a large and highly complex project:

- Scope: Exploring strange new worlds, seeking out new life and civilizations.
- Timeline: Five years.
- A unique undertaking: The original mission statement, "to boldly go where no one has gone before," emphasizes the unparalleled nature of the mission.

Throughout the series and subsequent films, we witnessed numerous instances where diversity played a crucial role in helping the team overcome dire situations. One notable example is found in Star Trek 2: The Wrath of Khan, where Spock, as the only individual capable of withstanding the radiation within the matter/antimatter chamber, was pivotal in initiating the Enterprise's engines. Others would have likely succumbed to the overwhelming conditions before the process could be completed.

So, how does diversity facilitate more effective risk management?

When identifying risks, relying solely on checklists and historical data may uncover some uncertainties, but it cannot replace the invaluable insights gained from a diverse range of knowledge. If team members and stakeholders possess similar educational backgrounds and experiences, critical risks are more likely to go unnoticed.

During risk analysis or when monitoring early warning signs of risk perception, diversity serves as an antidote to risk biases and groupthink, fostering more comprehensive assessments and responses.

Lastly, the quality of risk responses is inherently limited by the creativity and imagination of the team. Leveraging diversity, known to fuel greater creativity, opens up new possibilities for innovative risk mitigation strategies.

Therefore, the next time you confront a challenging project, resist the temptation to assemble a team composed solely of individuals who mirror your own perspectives. Instead, make diversity a primary criterion for resource selection, harnessing its power to unlock fresh insights and drive effective risk management.

Harnessing diversity creates a virtuous cycle alongside psychological safety.

The inclusion of diverse team compositions can greatly enhance risk identification. With varied backgrounds and experiences, team members often bring forth a broader range of risks that may be overlooked by a group lacking diversity. Moreover, diverse teams are acknowledged for their heightened creativity and potential for innovation. However, mere conceptual acceptance does not automatically translate into effective implementation.

Regrettably, inertia often prevails over diversity in team staffing. In matrix contexts, Project Managers communicate their skill requirements to personnel managers, who may prioritize securing individuals with the best skills for accomplishing the expected work. While the Project Manager may possess an underlying consideration for overall team diversity, the pressing demands faced by functional managers in fulfilling numerous concurrent talent requests can limit the inclusion of diversity as a search criterion. Even if the Project Manager wields greater power or influence, hesitancy in rejecting personnel recommendations from functional managers due to a lack of diversity may persist.

In projectized environments, Project Managers wield greater control over team selection. However, when pressured to meet aggressive deadlines, there may be a temptation to assemble the team as swiftly as possible, thereby relegating diversity to a secondary consideration.

Diversity quotas do not provide a comprehensive solution, as they can generate division rather than inclusivity. While oversight can provide some support, it cannot replace the authentic commitment of a Project Manager to deliberately build a diverse team.

Recruitment is merely the initial step. The opportunities presented by greater team diversity are squandered if inclusive practices are not embedded within the team's culture. A Project Manager's stance on conflict, for instance, influences their success in fostering inclusion. If conflict-avoidant, a Project Manager may inadvertently allow dominant voices to overshadow others within the team.

To promote genuine inclusion, we must begin by incorporating inclusivity in team agreements and actively model inclusive behaviors in our interactions. This topic could also be addressed during reflective sessions, encouraging team members to identify inclusive behaviors and actions, while raising awareness of those that may hinder inclusivity.

It is no coincidence that embracing diversity has been coupled with psychological safety as a primary tenet of the Disciplined Agile mindset. The more inclusive we are in embracing diversity within our teams, the greater the sense of safety experienced by team members. Consequently, team members feel more empowered to respect and encourage diverse perspectives, fostering a culture of innovation and growth.

Show me the money! (Diversity-oriented)

Last year (2020), PMI released its report "A Case for Diversity," which highlights the value of diversity for businesses. It contains several compelling facts, but let's focus on a few key ones:

- 88% of project leaders believe that teams with cultural and gender diversity enhance project value.
- 83% of project leaders believe that international team members contribute to increased project value.

These statistics represent significant majorities and should not be overlooked by any organization.

Around a year after the report's publication, many companies have embraced work models that continue to support distributed employees and teams to a much greater extent than before the pandemic. This presents unprecedented opportunities to embrace diverse teams. If the environment is conducive and leaders recognize the benefits it brings to projects, shouldn't embracing diversity be an obvious choice?

Projects thrive because of collaborative efforts - working together yields better solutions than individuals can achieve alone. Collaboration allows for the amalgamation of diverse backgrounds, skills, and experiences, leading to the development of enhanced solutions and approaches.

Consequently, it stands to reason that the greater the diversity and variety in individual backgrounds, the more diverse the collective collaboration will be. This, in turn, increases the likelihood of finding the best solution through collective teamwork. Whether teams are widely dispersed or fully remote, it is now easier to bring together people from underrepresented areas, whether geographically or culturally. This enhanced average diversity within a team also amplifies the team's chances of success. Team success translates to project success, ultimately benefiting businesses and delivering superior outcomes for organizations.

Supporting this notion, the PMI report reveals that organizations fostering gender-based programs tend to be more successful, as do those with culturally diverse leadership. As the world emerges from the profound recession caused by the pandemic, it is crucial for all to embrace the opportunity to enhance performance. However, the question remains: Is this commitment to diversity genuinely being realized?

The absence of strategic commitments

While many organizations can articulate statements highlighting the value of inclusion, equality, and diversity, it is important to scrutinize whether these words are substantiated by real actions.

Regrettably, the answer for many organizations today is "no." Despite previously having small-scale programs aimed at encouraging understanding and acceptance, these initiatives were among the first areas to face budget cuts during the pandemic-induced recession, and their restoration has yet to materialize in the majority of cases.

This is undeniably disheartening, but it also presents an opportunity. Small-scale tactical initiatives provide a semblance of progress, as any action is deemed better than none. However, such initiatives alone are insufficient to effect real change in how organizations approach diversity and equality issues. They also fail to generate improved return on investment (ROI) through a steadfast commitment to cultivating more diverse, project-based workforces.

What is truly required is a strategic commitment to diversity supported by substantial funding that drives these initiatives forward. This encompasses comprehensive educational and awareness programs for existing employees, alongside recruitment initiatives designed to make employers more appealing to a diverse range of candidates.

Concurrently, it necessitates a significant reduction in the proportion of white males holding executive positions, while fostering greater diversity within HR departments.

It is important to note that advocating for positive discrimination is not the intention here. Rather, the emphasis lies in organizations striving to select the most qualified individuals for each role. However, it is challenging to accept that nearly 90% of Fortune 500 CEOs, who are predominantly white males, solely attained their positions based on merit alone.

The Benefits of a Diversity-Driven Future

The world is entering a period of continuous and disruptive change. While we cannot predict the exact permanent changes that will result from COVID-19, we do know that the pandemic has transformed how, where, and when people work. Many organizations now recognize that distributed work can be more than just an effective operational model; it can also bring numerous benefits.

Additionally, the pandemic has accelerated digital transformation, leading to fundamental changes in how organizations operate and how individuals perceive work. As technology continues to evolve and redefine possibilities across various industries, customers constantly demand new and innovative solutions. Organizations that fail to deliver will risk losing business.

These circumstances place immense pressure on organizations to exceed the limits of what is possible, not only meeting customer demands but also anticipating them. Effective and efficient operational models are crucial. In essence, organizations must consistently offer the best solutions for each challenge they encounter.

This brings us back to the central point: diverse teams develop better solutions than homogeneous teams lacking diversity. Organizations, particularly in the private sector, are rapidly realizing that diversity is not merely a moral imperative or a competitive advantage, but rather a key element for sustainable business models.

However, it is essential to approach diversity intelligently. It is not simply about increasing representation of non-white or non-male individuals. It is not about tokenism or fulfilling quotas. As Steve Jobs once said, "It doesn't make sense to hire smart people and tell them what to do; we hire smart people so they can tell us what to do."

Intelligent diversity means hiring the best individuals, regardless of their background, from anywhere in the world. These individuals possess a wide range of skills, knowledge, and perspectives to help solve the organization's challenges. By allowing them to lead and contribute their unique insights, organizations can navigate the path to success.

This approach ensures that diversity is not the primary focus; instead, it becomes a natural outcome. When intelligent individuals with diverse backgrounds and experiences collaborate effectively, diversity becomes ingrained in the organizational culture. It transcends superficial checkboxes and leads to a true meritocracy. This is a significant departure from the current reality, where a disproportionate number of Fortune 500 CEOs are white males due to boardrooms predominantly composed of white males.

Simultaneously, embracing diversity fosters an environment where new ways of working are explored and adopted. Diverse teams think outside the box, pushing boundaries and generating innovative solutions. We witnessed this collective progress during the global collaboration on COVID-19 vaccine research. If we allow diverse perspectives to thrive, remarkable advancements are possible.

Organizations inherently understand that diversity drives performance. Collaboration has become commonplace, as diverse backgrounds and experiences lead to superior outcomes. However, the same progress has not been achieved when it comes to broader definitions of diversity. Often, performance goals are considered "good enough," or there is a lack of comprehension regarding the significant improvements achievable through a broader embrace of diversity.

In the increasingly competitive world we face, every advantage matters. Organizations across all industries must recognize that diversity, when thoughtfully implemented, acts as a catalyst for performance and success. It is not just a box to be checked but a strategic imperative for a thriving future.

Why do we make change so difficult when it can be simple?

At this point, it is well-established that projects are vehicles for change. They create new outcomes, enhance existing solutions, gradually improve current capabilities, or remove/correct underperforming assets. When a project is completed, something will be different when it emerges on the other side. Hopefully, the outcome is better in some way, but in all instances, the expectation is that it brings about some form of change.

This change can be a new business process or improvements to an existing one. It can produce a new transportation infrastructure. The change may involve digitizing a currently manual and inconsistent process. An organization may want to launch a new service offering. A manufacturer may want to build a new production line to improve automation. A company may construct new offices to support its operations. Utilizing these outcomes for their intended purpose creates circumstances where people are expected to work and interact differently than they did in the past.

Given this fundamental truth, you would think we would be very good at change by now. Unfortunately, we really aren't. In reality, change is often very, very poorly managed, to the extent that it is barely managed at all.

Many executives - and project managers, for that matter - believe that a logical justification for a new outcome will sell itself. If you create a compelling argument for the change, people will inherently appreciate the value of what is being implemented and adopt it wholesale.

That doesn't work. It has never worked. Despite this truth, organization after organization approaches the implementation of project outcomes - whether mundane or high-impact - as if it were an exercise in abstract logic and objective justification.

This logic may be what justifies the investment for the organization, of course. Whatever the value proposition offered in the business case, that may be reason enough for the organization to want to undertake the project. However, it by no means guarantees that the project outcomes will be persuasive or sufficiently desirable for the people who will use them.

Often, it is around this point that someone argues that if the change is important, senior management should simply compel people to do things the new way. The widespread assumption that this is an effective approach is frankly more than surprising. Yet, it is a statement that continues to be made, with the presumption that this is all that is needed for lasting and significant change to occur.

One of the most significant organizational change projects I provided consulting services for was an example of this. My role in the project was indirect, providing guidance on the planning process and how this project interacted with various others in the organization.

While the development of the technical solution was well thought out and meticulously defined, the initial assumption in the planning was that people would attend a short training course and radically change their work practices solely because the organization wanted it and the executive sponsor in charge would tell them they had to change.

Arguably, this is still a bit better than the organization that invested hundreds of thousands of dollars in system changes to implement a new program offering - only to send out a memo to their team that the system was ready and they should start delivering the program to their clients. There was literally no other communication. No training, no policy expectation, no process or procedure or guidance on how to manage the program. Just an email that the system was available, and everyone needed to go ahead and start using it.

Change as a phenomenon is incredibly simple. Organizations, executives, and project managers insist on making it tremendously difficult. You cannot drive change through logic and rational arguments. You cannot demand that people change. You cannot order them to work in a different way (well, you can... but it won't be very effective, and people will ignore, sabotage, or take shortcuts whenever they can). Change does not respond to orders, expectations, or whims. The very simple and straightforward bottom line is that change is about people. Successful change requires meeting people where they are and supporting them in transitioning to a new way of operating - to the extent that they buy into, accept, and value the outcomes. When they don't, change will not occur as expected or desired (certainly not without significant consequences).

The fact that change involves people is precisely why managers resort to logic, persuasion, or expectation, of course. It seems easier. Dealing with people is messy and difficult. It's frustrating. Different people have different reactions, want different things, and respond with different levels of support or hostility. It's much better and simpler to just force the change by telling people it's good for them or necessary, rather than the hard and complicated work of trying to convince them. The truth is, if you need people to work, interact, or behave differently than they do today, you will need to invest in supporting people as people. It's as simple as that. Doing so requires work and effort. There is no clear-cut, easily defined process to follow that guarantees success. You will need to adjust, adapt, and course-correct along the way.

It will take longer than you imagine and require more iterations and reinforcement than you believe reasonable. Doing so - through all the complicated pathways you will traverse - is still the most direct path possible if what you want is real change.

While there is no direct process, there are essential principles to guide you. They are universal, meaningful, and surprisingly constant and enduring. One of these principles is grounded in how change needs to be communicated. You need to build a case for change. However, this is not a business case based on numbers and logic. It is a credible narrative that addresses some fundamental and material questions:

What is being done? The first and fundamental question is the identification of what is being done. It must be specific and concrete. It should describe the actual outcome that will occur. It should describe what will happen in the clearest and simplest terms possible. It should avoid abstract descriptions and flowery jargon. You are not "seeking long-term synergy and strategic alignment"; you are "acquiring our next biggest competitor and merging their operations with ours over the next nine months."

Why is it being done? Secondly, be clear about why the change is being made. Again, this should be straightforward. It should also be honest. This is as close as you will get to the orbit of the business case, but what is described needs to be specific. This is not a sales pitch. It is a sincere explanation of why what is being done is important from the organization's standpoint.

What will be different? Next, be absolutely clear about what will change as a result of the project. You may have fewer branches, or job roles and functions may be different, or customers may interact online and through call centers instead of in-person, or decisions will now be automated and consistent rather than left to the team's discretion. This should be framed more directly around the changes people will see and experience as a consequence of the project.

What will remain the same? As important as defining the change is identifying what will not change. If left unaddressed, people will imagine larger implications than you may intend. Being clear about what will still be the same going forward is an important foundation for people to work from. It allows people to assess the magnitude of the impact that will occur and find comfort in what will still be familiar.

What's in it for me? The last and most important question is how the change will make a difference for the people being asked to make adjustments. It is not about abstract organizational benefits but real personal impacts. How will personal experiences improve as a result of changing to the new way of operating? How will they be better off or better? In what ways will people who make the change be more successful?

You can look at the last point in particular and ask, **"What if there is no significant benefit for them?"** The simple answer to that question is that the change will fail. If the improvements do not make the lives of the people being asked to make the change better, the change will not happen. It will be resisted, sabotaged, and at best paid lip service. It may not be obvious that the change is failing at first, but it certainly will be.

Let's imagine, for example, that you are implementing a new system that will automate a currently manual process. The reason for doing this is that the current approach is complicated, inconsistently followed, and time-consuming. The new approach will impose rules, ensure consistency, apply decision rules uniformly, and require little attention and effort from the staff. From the organizational perspective, the value is clear: efficiency, cost savings, fewer staff, and consistent decisions.

From the perspective of the people managing the current process, there is very little gain and a lot of loss. They may fear losing their jobs. They may see it as a threat to their expertise. They may resent having less interaction with customers. They may see it as something that hinders their ability to serve their customers well. They may see it turning their advisory role into a glorified clerk. In fact, they will probably think of all these things and more.

How they will respond will depend on where they are in terms of roles, careers, and personal mobility. Some may hunker down and hope for the best. Others may actively undermine or even openly sabotage the solution. Still, others will put their resumes out on the street as soon as the winds of change blow for the first time. There is nothing in this that appears to embrace, accept, or value what is being done because there is nothing being done that results in a better situation for the people.

The essential principle of all change is that people need to see themselves as more successful using the new way than anything they currently do. Their lives need to materially improve in ways that are specifically important to them. What is being implemented needs to be an improvement that they personally see. This means that any change, to be embraced by the people who will use it, needs to be designed to deliver that improvement.

You need to take the time to understand what matters today. You need to learn what is valued in current roles and the sources of frustration and friction. You need to make time to explore what "better" would look like and how to do that in a way that would be valued and adopted.

This takes work. It takes effort. It puts the people responsible for the work of the process in the driver's seat. Which should not surprise anyone. If they are being asked to do the work and deliver the outcomes, they need solutions and support that allow them to be more successful in delivering that value. It may well mean simplifying and automating aspects of a process that are barriers and inefficiencies. The intent is that, by doing so, people can be more successful in doing the things that make a difference.

Change is simple. The only change that works is done with people, not to people. The only change that is accepted is one that leaves people in a better position, in ways and means that are important to them. Design for making a difference to the people doing the work first, if you want any hope of improvements being embraced and real change occurring. It's as simple... and as difficult as that.

9 PROJECT MANAGEMENT AND GOVERNANCE

Project governance is the management framework within which project decisions are made. Project governance is a critical element of any project, as the responsibilities associated with the business of an organization as usual activities are established in its organizational governance agreements; there is rarely an equivalent structure to govern the development of its capital investments (projects). For example, the organizational chart provides a good indication of who in the organization is responsible for any specific operational activity the organization conducts. But unless an organization has specifically developed a project governance policy, such a chart is likely nonexistent for project development activity.

Therefore, the role of project governance is to provide a logical, robust, and repeatable decision-making framework to govern an organization's capital investments. In this way, an organization will have a structured approach to conduct its business-as-usual activities and its business changes or project activities.

Basic Principles of Project Governance

Principle 1: Ensure a single point of responsibility for project success

The fundamental responsibility of a project is its success. A project without a clear understanding of who is accountable for its success lacks effective leadership. Without clear accountability for project success, there is no one driving the resolution of the challenging problems that arise during the project lifecycle. This also hinders the project during the crucial initiation phase, as there is no one making important decisions to establish a solid foundation. The concept of a single point of responsibility is the first principle of effective project governance.

However, it is not sufficient to simply assign someone as accountable; the right person must be held responsible. There are two aspects to consider. The responsible person must have sufficient authority within the organization to make necessary decisions for project success. Additionally, the individual selected must come from the appropriate area within the organization. Choosing the wrong person leaves the project no better off than having no one accountable for its success. The only person who can assume responsibility for project success is the focus of Principle 1.

Principle 2: Project ownership separate from asset ownership, service ownership, or other stakeholder groups

Organizations often allocate project ownership to the owner of the service or asset, aiming to ensure that the project meets the fundamental needs of that owner, which is a critical measure of project success. However, this approach can lead to unnecessary scope inclusions and failure to address alternative requirements from stakeholders and the client:

- The benefit of the doubt favors the stakeholder assigned project ownership, distorting the project outcome.
- The project owner's requirements receive less scrutiny, reducing innovation and efficiency.
- Different skill sets are involved in project ownership, asset ownership, and service ownership, jeopardizing decision-making and project procedures.
- Operational needs always take precedence, risking neglect of the project during those times.

Project contingencies risk being allocated as additional scope to the stakeholder-assigned project ownership.

The only proven mechanism to ensure projects meet customer and stakeholder needs, optimizing the cost-benefit relationship, is to assign project ownership to a specialized party who would otherwise not be a stakeholder in the project. This is Principle 2 of project governance. The project owner is engaged with clear terms that describe the organization's key outcome areas and the organization's perspective on the project's key stakeholders. Organizations often establish a Project

Governance Committee, which identifies projects and appoints project owners early in the project's life, establishes Project Boards for customer and stakeholder involvement, sets key outcome areas consistent with the organization's values, and oversees project performance. These parameters are commonly detailed in a Project Governance Plan that remains in effect throughout the project's duration (distinct from a more detailed Project Management Plan that is developed during project execution).

Projects have multiple stakeholders, and effective project governance should address their needs. The next principle addresses how this should be done.

Principle 3: Ensure separation of stakeholder management and project decision-making activities

The effectiveness of a committee's decision-making is inversely proportional to its size. Large committees not only struggle to make timely decisions but often make poorly considered decisions due to specific group dynamics.

As project decision-making forums grow in size, they tend to become stakeholder management forums. With increased numbers, participants' detailed understanding of critical project issues decreases. Many attendees are present to stay informed rather than actively contribute to decision-making. There is insufficient time for each person to present their viewpoint, and those with valuable input must compete for limited time and influence with those less involved in the project. Furthermore, not all attendees will have the same level of understanding, wasting time on bringing everyone up to speed on specific issues. Consequently, large project committees resemble stakeholder management forums rather than decision-making bodies. Undoubtedly, both stakeholder management and project decision-making are essential for project success. However, they are distinct activities and should be treated as such. This is the third principle of effective project governance. Achieving this separation avoids clogging decision-making forums with numerous stakeholders, limiting participation to essential stakeholders selected for their contribution to success.

There is always a concern that this solution may create another problem if dissatisfied stakeholders feel their needs are not being met.

Whatever stakeholder management mechanism is implemented, it must adequately address the needs of all project stakeholders. It should capture their input and viewpoints and satisfactorily address their concerns. One approach is to have stakeholder groups chaired by the Project Board Chairman, ensuring stakeholders have the project owner (or SRO) to advocate for their issues and concerns within the Project Board.

Principle 4: Ensure separation of project governance and organizational governance structures

Project governance structures are established precisely because it is recognized that organizational structures do not provide the necessary framework for project delivery. Projects require flexibility and agility in decision-making, which hierarchical mechanisms associated with organizational charts do not support. Project governance structures overcome this by removing key decision-makers from the organizational structure and placing them in a forum, thus avoiding the serial decision-making process of hierarchies.

Therefore, the project governance structure established for a project must remain separate from the organizational structure. It is acknowledged that the organization has valid reporting and stakeholder involvement requirements. However, dedicated reporting mechanisms established by the project can address reporting needs, while the project governance structure should address stakeholder involvement. What should be avoided is the need for decisions made by the project governance committee or project board to be ratified by individuals from the organization outside the project's decision-making forum. Either include these individuals as members of the project's decision-making body or empower the existing governance committee/project board. The governance committee/project board is responsible for approving, reviewing progress, and delivering the project's intended outcomes and benefits. Therefore, they must have decision-making authority, including resource allocation and funding adjustments beyond the original plan. This is the final principle of effective project governance. Adopting this principle minimizes decision-making layers and the associated delays and inefficiencies. It ensures a project decision-making body with the power to make timely decisions.

Corporate Governance is at the core of good ESG practices in companies, and here's why

The topic of corporate responsibility related to the environmental and social sustainability of businesses has been prominent for some time. What changes in the current pursuit of ESG practices is the pressure from investors. It is in this context that the pillar of Corporate Governance stands out, as it provides the consistency and viability for all sustainable projects that a company undertakes.

Corporate Governance organizes the principles and processes of managing a company to ensure compliance with laws and regulations, with a focus on good performance. It is through Corporate Governance that stakeholders such as employees, suppliers, shareholders, and investors are connected.

In the current scenario of climate crisis and intensifying discussions on human rights, companies need to implement governance systems guided by a vision of their social role. They are being expected to demonstrate commitment to actions that ensure their long-term relevance, beyond immediate profitability.

What is the role of Corporate Governance?

Corporate governance acts as the guiding thread that runs through all operations and relationships within a company, ensuring the fulfillment of its strategic planning while minimizing negative impacts and maximizing positive results. This includes applying transparency in processes, ensuring objectivity and information flows for all involved parties, establishing trust both internally and externally.

One aspect related to transparency is accountability. This pertains to financial matters, such as the integrity of transactions, accuracy of profit and expense figures, payment of taxes and social obligations, as well as the results of initiatives aimed at improving social and environmental indicators.

Increasingly attentive to risks related to ESG criteria, shareholders and investors rely on the sound governance structure of companies for the success of their businesses.

How Governance impacts ESG

Governance is the foundation of all ESG initiatives, practices, and projects. Firstly, it ensures cohesion between any company undertaking and the objectives of the business. Therefore, it is crucial that governance is aligned with a vision of sustainable development. Furthermore, governance establishes standards and criteria that shape the organizational culture.

When developed based on sustainable development principles, governance should prioritize ethics and transparency, aiming for decision-making that considers social well-being and the environment. Cases of corruption, data breaches of customers and employees, accidents, violation of environmental permits, prejudice, and discrimination are some of the risks resulting from a lack of commitment to governance.

Valuing human integrity and ecosystems is a key aspect of governance that supports the implementation of ESG as an integral part of business practices. This sets it apart from actions that inadequately address the impacts of company activities and may, therefore, be ineffective or poorly regarded by the public.

Governance Solutions for ESG Projects

Investors pay attention to various indices that allow them to evaluate and monitor companies' performance in relation to their socio-environmental commitments. These indices assess aspects such as corporate sustainability management, risk management, business ethics, compliance with legal and regulatory criteria, diversity and inclusion in the workforce and top management, among others.

Being in compliance with all these aspects should not be seen as an isolated challenge. Instead, it is an ongoing journey of adjustment and continuous monitoring. To achieve this, each company needs customized tools and solutions to optimize the governance of its business.

Governance of Innovation in Portfolios, Programs, and Projects

The importance of governance in Portfolios, Programs, and Projects (3P) is reflected, in part, by the development of governance standards, as well as the increasing attention given to governance in academic and managerial literature and practice. At the same time, organizations are increasingly aiming to enhance their innovation capabilities, enabling them to survive in today's dynamic and competitive environment. However, there is limited guidance in research literature on whether and how 3P governance can be designed to support and promote innovation. The growing significance of project delivery in organizations, particularly for innovation, further highlights the need for a better understanding of the relationship between governance, innovation, and success in 3P.

Governance is becoming increasingly important for the success of 3Ps from an organizational perspective, and several studies have highlighted the need for governance to be appropriate for the environment. Large-scale studies demonstrate that effective executive management oversight fosters and nurtures innovation. However, some studies also suggest that it can lead to negative tension, as innovation requires flexible and adaptable approaches.

Embracing Governance as an Asset

I'm not sure any project manager will tell you they love organizational governance functions. Whether it's process governance applied by the PMO or a project steering committee aimed at ensuring the project delivers what is needed, there's always a sense that someone is checking the project manager and possibly questioning their decisions.

For new project managers, this can sometimes be even more challenging than for those with more experience. Their projects tend to be less significant to the organization, and they may not have formal management oversight or a supervisory committee. This can result in less formal governance, especially as things like process audits are becoming less common (a topic for another day), and instead, there are simple inquiries from sponsors and clients.

If you're a new project manager struggling to figure out how to be successful and finding that your actions are being questioned, it's easy to become discouraged. But you shouldn't be – governance can be your ally!

Understanding the Purpose of Governance

Let's take a step back for a minute and consider why governance exists. It's not because people are untrustworthy, but because having more than one person monitoring performance makes it more likely that any issues or errors will be detected earlier. And the sooner we find a problem, the easier it is to fix.

Let's also acknowledge that governance is not something that only happens at relatively low levels of organizations. Executives are subject to more forms of governance than virtually any other function, and organizations themselves are subject to a range of formal governance processes regularly.

As project managers, we should, therefore, embrace governance functions. They can help ensure our projects are successful by identifying issues we may overlook, providing a different perspective on the available information, and offering alternative ideas for addressing challenges.

But the key here is "can." They have the potential to do this, but sometimes the way governance is applied means it doesn't happen. Instead, governance may seem to judge us as individuals, questioning our ability to manage projects. If this occurs, it is up to project managers to address it.

Governance Working with Project Management, Not Against It
Project managers should view governance as something they work with to improve outcomes. If project managers feel that governance is being imposed on them rather than working collaboratively with them, then something needs to change. And I hope project managers will respond if that's the case.

There is a perception in some organizations that governance is something that cannot be questioned, that decisions simply need to be accepted. But it is not an independent audit, nor is it something supported by legislative or regulatory structures – it is merely a form of management oversight.

I know questioning management is not always a good career move, but the only reason governance should exist is to make things better. Therefore, if it is not focused on that goal, project managers need to steer it in the right direction.

Based on conversations with colleagues, I can share an example to illustrate the point. One consultant was working in an organization where there was a clear disagreement in the steering committee about whether their presence was necessary. The committee chair had hired them, while other members believed that the organization's staff was capable of handling the project.

During a steering committee meeting in the chair's absence, it became evident from the start that this would be an opportunity to criticize every decision, action taken, and interpretation made regarding the project's status. The consultant listened to the criticisms for a long time, and when it was over, simply thanked the committee for the feedback and asked for guidance on where they believed the project should go now. They had nothing to offer.

In reality, this was more of a steering committee than a governance committee, and it clarifies what the function should be. Its purpose is to guide the project in the right direction if it veers off track. Looking back and questioning every turn and adjustment made is one thing, but that is not direction.

If the direction the project was taking needed to change, then that should be discussed and understood why. The objective should always be to improve project performance – exactly what governance should aim to achieve.

Can governance be beneficial? Governance should be beneficial. And project managers should embrace the concept as a way to enhance project performance. However, if governance ends up being merely an opportunity to criticize the project manager's performance and decision-making, then project managers must be able to step back and insist that the focus remains on creating the best possible project delivery environment.

Project Governance, Risk, and Compliance: Finding the Right Balance

There is a delicate balance between having excessively burdensome project governance and having insufficient governance. Too much governance can hinder productivity and stifle creativity. The focus shifts towards complying with checklists and form submissions, rather than maintaining momentum and striving to achieve project goals.

On the other hand, too little governance can allow defects to enter the project management process, increasing the risk of budget and time overruns, as well as an elevated rate of failures. Finding the optimal level of governance, risk management, and compliance is crucial for a successful Project Management Office (PMO).

Having led projects in both loosely regulated PMOs and overly stringent ones, I can confidently say that I prefer the former. Let's face it: if you have skilled project managers, they are usually self-governed and thrive in an environment that allows for creativity. While under-managing them may pose some risks, it can also lead to impressive successes.

However, if your project management team is average, lacking strong leadership and administrative skills, it becomes essential to maintain a firm grip on governance to prevent projects from going off track.

The project management community agrees that the best approach to Governance, Risk, and Compliance (GRC) is to incorporate compliance metrics into the regular project management process rather than burdening project managers with additional reporting tasks that they often resist. One way to achieve this is through the automation of certain GRC aspects.

For instance, if the project team updates progress against project plans or sprint boards, this data should automatically feed into timelines, project accounting information, and other relevant data sources. Another effective strategy is to assign tasks with limited duration and effort (one to three days), ensuring that each assignment produces verifiable work deliverables. This eliminates the need for subjective estimates of task completion percentages. Instead, tasks are considered either completed or not. With shorter durations, any deviations from the plan can be promptly identified and addressed.

Another approach to reduce the burden of GRC while maintaining high-quality project processes is to continually recalibrate the project plan to reflect the evolving path ahead. This recalibration allows project managers to focus on the next two to four weeks of work products, keeping the team aligned with the project's overall goals and objectives. As long as the project remains within the designated budget and delivery timeline, there is no need for excessive and intrusive oversight.

Instead, the PMO can concentrate on addressing plan deviations and exceptions, avoiding a one-size-fits-all approach. The underlying project management/tracking system should provide analysis and insights into plan deviations, enabling the PMO to take proactive measures to get projects back on track.

It is essential to remember that the role of the PMO is to consistently manage and deliver project assets in a timely and cost-effective manner. The primary goal is to realize project benefits as early as possible. Every aspect of the PMO's activities, from rules and protocols to compliance guidelines, should be evaluated against this objective. Any elements that fail to contribute to this goal should be eliminated from the GRC process.

In summary, providing effective governance through the PMO does not have to be a daunting task. By establishing a framework that supports success and enables proactive oversight, the PMO can strike the right balance between governance, risk management, and compliance, fostering a productive and innovative project environment.

10 REFERENCES

The GPM P5 Standard for Sustainability in Project Management Portuguese (BR) Version 2.0

2022 Insights into Sustainable Project Management

2015SDG_Compass_2issues_doc_Financial_markets_who_cares_who_wins

Applying the P5 Standard for Sustainability: Enriching Project Leadership - EJ van Rooyen - University of Limpopo, South Africa

https://www.projectmanagement.com

https://kbondale.wordpress.com

https://www.pmi.org/learning/thought-leadership/megatrends

https://ambipar.com/latam/pt/noticias/esg-o-que-e-governanca/

ABOUT THE AUTHOR

If you've reached this point, I want to thank you for your interest and congratulate you for wanting your projects, or the projects you're involved in, to be sustainable in all aspects, not just the environment.

I've been a project manager for over a decade, leading projects across Latin America. After a lot of learning and experimenting, I saw that this is a path of no return: there is no way to stop learning when it comes to Project Management.

I am PMP certified since 2015 and GPM-b since 2020.

I also work part-time as a professor at the University of Campinas - UNICAMP - Brazil since 2015, teaching about Project Management.

This is my fourth authorial project where I write about the area and invite you to discover my other works or connect to LinkedIn.

Finally, I am Angelica's husband, Benjamin's father and a storyteller...